A NARRATIVE

OF THE

EXPERIENCE AND SUFFERINGS

OF

WILLIAM DODD,

A FACTORY CRIPPLE.

WRITTEN BY HIMSELF.

GIVING AN ACCOUNT OF THE HARDSHIPS AND SUFFERINGS HE ENDURED IN EARLY LIFE, UNDER WHAT DIFFICULTIES HE ACQUIRED HIS EDUCATION, THE EFFECTS OF FACTORY LABOUR ON HIS MIND AND PERSON, THE UNSUCCESSFUL EFFORTS MADE BY HIM TO OBTAIN A LIVELIHOOD IN SOME OTHER LINE OF LIFE, THE COMPARISON HE DRAWS BETWEEN AGRICULTURAL AND MANUFACTURING LABOURERS, AND OTHER MATTERS RELATING TO THE WORKING CLASSES.

SECOND EDITION.

LONDON:

PUBLISHED BY L. & G. SEELEY, 169, FLEET STREET,
AND HATCHARD & SON, 187, PICCADILLY.

1841.

PRICE ONE SHILLING.

TO

LORD ASHLEY, M.P.

MY LORD,

The sympathy you were pleased to express for me, after seeing a brief outline of my sufferings, and witnessing the effects of the factory system on my person, and believing that a more extensive circulation of my narrative may, under Providence, be the means of assisting the strenuous exertions your Lordship is making on behalf of that oppressed class of work-people to which I belong, I have been induced to prepare for the press an enlarged and corrected account, to be issued in a separate form; and beg, as a token of gratitude, to dedicate these, my humble endeavours, to you, who are so thoroughly conversant with the momentous subject to which my remarks refer.

And am,

MY LORD,

Your Lordship's

Much obliged,

Humble Servant,

WILLIAM DODD.

23, Little Gray's Inn Lane,
June 18, 1841.

A NARRATIVE, &c.

Dear Reader,—I wish it to be distinctly and clearly understood, that, in laying before you the following sheets, I am not actuated by any motive of ill-feeling to any party with whom I have formerly been connected; on the contrary, I have a personal respect for some of my former masters, and am convinced that, had they been in any other line of life, they would have shone forth as ornaments to the age in which they lived; but having witnessed the efforts of some writers (who can know nothing of the factories by experience) to mislead the minds of the public upon a subject of so much importance, I feel it to be my duty to give to the world a fair and impartial account of the working of the factory system, as I have found it in twenty-five years' experience.

I cannot, at this distance of time, take upon myself to say what were the predisposing circumstances by which my parents were induced to send their children to the factories, especially as I was very young at the time my eldest sister first went, and cannot be supposed then to have known much of their affairs. I shall, therefore, confine myself, in the following narrative, to such facts as may serve to show the *effects* of the system upon my mind, person, and condition.

Of four children in our family, I was the only boy; and we were all at different periods, as we could meet with employers, sent to work in the factories. My eldest sister was ten years of age before she went; consequently, she was, in a manner, out of harm's way, her bones having become firmer and stronger than ours, and capable of withstanding the hardships to which she was exposed much better than we could: but her services soon became more valuable in another line of industry. My second sister went at the age of seven years, and, like myself, has been made a cripple for life, and doomed to end her days in the factories or workhouse. My youngest sister also went early, but was obliged to be taken away, like many more, the work being too hard for her! although she afterwards stood a very hard service.

I was born on the 18th of June, 1804; and in the latter part of 1809, being then turned of five years of age, I was put to work at card-making, and about a year after I was sent, with my sisters, to the factories. I was then a fine, strong, healthy, hardy boy, straight in every limb, and remarkably stout and active. It was predicted by many of our acquaintance, that I should be the very model of my father, who was the picture of robust health and strength, and, in his time, had been the don of the village, and had carried off the prize at almost every manly sport.

A circumstance occurred between my fifth and sixth year, which places the fact of my being strong and active beyond a doubt. I was then about getting my first boy's dress of trousers and jacket, and, being stout, I had long felt ashamed of my petticoats, and was very glad when I heard that a friend had offered to supply my parents with the necessary articles of dress for me, giving them a sufficient length of time for payment. This friend lived at the distance of three-quarters of a mile from our house; and I well remember going with my eldest sister for my clothes. There was a great quantity of ready-made dresses, one of which being selected and tried on, the tailor thought it was rather too little; but I thought it would do very well, especially as it had got a watch-pocket in it; and not liking the idea of losing what I had got, or of having again to wear the petticoats, I ran out of the shop, and did not stop till I had got home, my sister calling after, but not being able to overtake me. I was put into the factories soon after, and have never been able to perform this feat of running three-quarters of a mile since.

From six to fourteen years of age, I went through a series of uninterrupted, unmitigated suffering, such as very rarely falls to the lot of mortals so early in life, except to those situated as I was, and such as I could not have withstood, had I not been strong, and of a good constitution.

My first place in the factories was that of piecer, or the lowest situation; but as the term conveys only a vague idea of the duties to be performed, it will be necessary here to give such explanation as may enable those unacquainted with the business to form a just conception of what those duties are, and to judge of the inadequacy of the remuneration or reward for their performance, and the cruelty of the punishments inflicted for the neglect of those duties. The duties of a piecer in the cotton, worsted, and woollen mills, differ considerably, but their rewards and punishments are very much alike. What I shall have to say in the following pages, must be understood to relate to the woollen mills only, which is, on all hands, allowed to be the best for the piecer. It is in this situation of piecer that the greatest number of cripples are made from over-exertion.

The duties of the piecer will not be clearly understood by the reader, unless he is previously made acquainted with the machine for spinning woollen yarn, called a *Billy*. I must, therefore, crave his patience, till I make this matter as clear as I am able. A billy, then, is a machine somewhat similar in form to the letter H, one side being stationary, and the other moveable, and capable of being pushed close in under the stationary part, almost like the drawer of a side table; the moveable part, or carriage, runs backwards and forwards, by means of six iron wheels, upon three iron rails, as a carriage on a railroad. In this carriage are the spindles, from 70 to 100 in number, all turned by one wheel, which is in the care of the spinner. When the spinner brings the carriage close up under the fixed part of the machine, he is able, by a contrivance for that purpose, to obtain a certain length of carding for each spindle, say 10 or 12 inches, which he draws back, and spins into yarn; this done, he winds the yarn round the spindles, brings the carriage close up as before, and again obtains a fresh supply of cardings. The side of the billy appropriated to the piecers is composed of a number of boards set in a slanting direction the whole length, somewhat like the face of a writing-desk; over these boards are put cloths made of coarse wrapper, in the form of a jack-towel, only not so long, and much wider. These cloths move on two rollers, one at the top, and one at the bottom of the slanting board; and by this means the cardings, which are laid in parallel lines thereon, are conveyed, as they are wanted, to the points of the spindles. On the top of the cardings, and immediately over the upper roller, runs the billy-roller—the dreaded instrument of punishment for the children. This roller is very easily taken out and put in its place, and is at the full command of the spinner, and, being of great length, it is scarcely possible for the piecer to get out of the way, should the spinner think proper to give him a knock. On these coarse canvas cloths the piecer pieces the ends of the cardings, and prepares them for the spinner.

The cardings are strips of wool 27 inches long, and of equal thickness throughout, (generally about as thick as a lady's finger,) except about 2 inches at each end, which are smaller, in order that when two ends are laid one over the other, and rubbed together with the piecer's flat hand, the piecing may not be thicker than any other part of the carding.

These cardings are taken up by the piecer in his left hand, about 20 at a time. He holds them in nearly the same manner as a joiner would hold a bunch of ornamental shavings for a parlour fire-place, about 4 inches from one end, the other end hanging down; these he takes, with his right hand, one at a time, for the purpose of piecing, and, laying the ends of the cardings about 2 inches over each other, he rubs them together on the canvas cloth with his flat hand. He is obliged to be very expert, in order to keep the spinner well supplied. A good piecer will supply from 30 to 40 spindles with cardings; but this depends, in a great measure, upon the quality of the work to be done, and also whether it is intended for the warp or the weft of the cloth to be made.

The cloths upon which the piecer rubs, or pieces, the ends of the cardings, as above stated, are made of coarse wrappering. The number of cardings a piecer has through his fingers in a day is very great; each piecing requires three or four rubs, over a space of three or four inches; and the continual friction of the hand in rubbing the piecing upon the coarse wrapper wears off the skin, and causes the fingers to bleed. I have had my fingers in this state for weeks together, healing up in the night, and breaking out again in little holes as soon as I commenced work on the following morning.

Another source of pain in the hands of piecers, is their continually swelling from cold in the winter season; and this is an evil which, like the other, cannot altogether be prevented. In a future page, I shall have to describe the process of oiling the wool; at present, it will be enough to say, that the oil gets rubbed into the cloths upon which the cardings are pieced, and, as a matter of course, the cloths get black, greasy, and cold. With continually passing over these comfortless things, the hands get cold, and swell very much; and as there is but little, and in many places no fire allowed, it is next to impossible for them to keep their hands warm; add to this the clothes they have upon their backs, are generally as greasy and comfortless as those upon which they piece, and stick to their arms, legs, and thighs, more like a wet sack than anything intended for warmth and comfort.

The position in which the piecer stands to his work is

with his right foot forward, and his right side facing the frame: the motion he makes in going along in front of the frame, for the purpose of piecing, is neither forwards nor backwards, but in a sidling direction, constantly keeping his right side towards the frame. In this position he continues during the day, with his hands, feet, and eyes constantly in motion. It will be easily seen, that the chief weight of his body rests upon his right knee, which is almost always the first joint to give way. The number of cripples with the right knee in, greatly exceed those with the left knee in; a great many have both knees in—such as my own—from this cause.

Another evil resulting from the position in which the piecer stands, is what is termed " splay-foot," which may be explained thus: in a well-formed foot, there is a finely formed arch of bones immediately under the instep and ankle joint. The continual pressure of the body on this arch, before it is sufficiently strong to bear such pressure, (as in the case of boys and girls in the factories,) causes it to give way; the bones fall gradually down, the foot then becomes broad and flat, and the owner drags it after him with the broad side first. A great many factory cripples are in this state; this is very often attended with weak ankle and knee joints. I have a brother-in-law exactly thus, who has tried every thing likely to do him good, but without success.

The spinner and the piecer are intimately connected together: the spinner works by the piece, being paid by the stone for the yarn spun; the piecer is hired by the week, and paid according to his abilities. The piecers are the servants of the spinners, and both are under an overlooker, and liable to be dismissed at a week's notice. Being thus circumstanced, it is clearly the advantage of the spinner to have good able piecers, who ought, in return, to be well paid. At my first starting in the works, I had 1s. per week, and got gradually advanced till I was 14 years old, at which time I had 3s. 6d. per week. The average wages are about 2s. 6d.; and thus, for a sum of money varying from one farthing to one halfpenny per hour, a sum not more than half sufficient to find me in necessaries, I was compelled, under fear of the strap and the billy-roller, (the smart of which I had often been made to feel—with the force of the latter, I have been struck almost motionless on the factory floor!) to keep in active employ, although my hands were frequently swollen, and the blood was dripping from my fingers' ends. I was also compelled to listen to, and be witness of almost every species of immorality, debauchery, and wickedness; and finally, to be deprived of the power of those faculties nature had so bountifully supplied me with.

In order to induce the piecer to do his work quick and well, the spinner has recourse to many expedients, such as offering rewards of a penny or two-pence for a good week's work—inducing them to sing, which, like the music in the army, has a very powerful effect, and keeps them awake and active longer than any other thing ; and, as a last resource, when nothing else will do, he takes the strap, or the billy-roller, which are laid on most unmercifully, accompanied by a round volley of oaths; and I pity the poor wretch who has to submit to the infliction of either.

On one occasion, I remember being thrashed with the billy-roller till my back, arms, and legs were covered with ridges as thick as my finger. This was more than I could bear, and, seeing a favourable opportunity, I slipped out, and stole off home, along some by-ways, so as not to be seen. Mother stripped me, and was shocked at my appearance. The spinner, not meeting with any other to suit him, had the assurance to come and beg that mother would let me go again, and promised not to strike me with the billy-roller any more. He kept his promise, but instead of using the roller, he used his fist.

Another ignorant brute of a spinner whom I pieced for, had a great inclination to use his hand as an instrument of punishment. One time, when I was sleepy and tired, and did not keep my ends right, he struck me a blow on the side of the head, which made me reel about, and it was some time before I recovered myself. It was a great mercy I was not taken in by the machinery. For a long time after, I cherished a sort of revenge, and could not look upon the brute without remembering the blow, and used to say within myself, only let me get to be a man, and then I will pay you with interest. I am glad, however, to hear that he has since learned to read, and has become a worthy member of society. Should he see this, he may rest assured he has my forgiveness.

A piecer, it will be seen, is an important person in the factories, inasmuch as it is impossible to do without them. Formerly, boys and girls were sent to work in the factories as piecers, at the early age of five or six years—as in my own case—but now, owing to the introduction of some wise laws for the regulation of factories, they cannot employ any as piecers before they have attained the age of 9 years; at which age their bones are comparatively strong, generally speaking, and more able to endure the hardships to which they will be exposed.

They now enjoy many privileges that we had not, such as attending schools, limited hours of labour, &c.; but still it is far from being a desirable place for a child. Formerly, it was nothing but work till we could work no longer. I have frequently worked at the frame till I could scarcely get home, and in this state have been stopped by people in the streets who noticed me shuffling along, and advised me to work no more in the factories: but I was not my own master. Thus year after year passed away, my afflictions and deformities increasing. I could not associate with any body; on the contrary, I sought every opportunity to rest myself, and to shrink into any corner to screen myself from the prying eye of the curious and scornful! During the day, I frequently counted the clock, and calculated how many hours I had still to remain at work; my evenings were spent in preparing for the following day—in rubbing my knees, ankles, elbows, and wrists with oil, &c., and wrapping them in warm flannel! (for everything was tried to benefit me, except the right one—*that of taking me from the work ;)* after which, with a *look at*, rather than *eating* my supper, (the bad smells of the factory having generally taken my appetite away,) I went to bed, to cry myself to sleep, and pray that the Lord would take me to himself before morning.

Even Sunday—that day of rest to the weary and oppressed—shone no Sabbath day for me; for, although I was no longer urged on and kept in motion by the fear of the strap and the billy-roller, yet the leisure thus afforded to think and reflect upon my situation, only made me the more miserable!—If Sunday was bad, Monday morning was still worse—it was horrible! Even now, it makes me tremble, to think upon the sufferings of those mornings! My joints were then like so many rusty hinges, that had laid by for years. I had to get up an hour earlier, and, with the broom under one arm as a crutch, and a stick in my hand, walk over the house till I had got my joints into working order! and then, this day of the week was generally the most painful of the seven.

I frequently pressed my parent to get me something else to do, as I was anxious to leave the factories, and to get some work more tolerable. I got two engagements. At one place, they kept me a week, and the other only about a quarter of an hour. This latter circumstance is still fresh in my memory. I was engaged to be an errand boy to an ironmonger. This engagement was made without him seeing me; and, when he did see me, on account of my deformity, he expressed his fears I should not be able to do his work, but said I might try. On this morning, I had been drilling myself longer than usual on my crutch, and the hopes of getting from the factories had made me tolerably active! So, I set to work, to take down the shop-shutters, as he directed me. There was one step up, from the street into the shop; and, having got one of the shutters down, and on my shoulder, I was about to make this step — but it proved too much for me, and I fell beneath the load! My master seeing this, told me I was of no service to him, gave me three-pence, and dismissed me!

Judge what my feelings must have been at this time; after fancying myself on the point of leaving for ever a place wherein I had suffered so much, and then to see all my hopes dashed to the ground, and I sent back to what appeared to me the most hateful place on earth—the factories!

I have above alluded to the bad smells of the factories, which any one, who has ever been in or near a factory, must have noticed; and I shall here endeavour to explain what is the cause of those smells. If we examine a pile or fibre of wool through a microscope, we find it has a very uneven appearance, being notched or indented along its surface, somewhat similar to the teeth of a saw. It is this unevenness of surface, that causes the fibres to unite closely and firmly together in the formation of cloths, hats, &c.; but although it is ultimately an advantage, it presents an obstacle to the manufacturer, which he is obliged to overcome in the following manner:—

When the wool is sorted into the different qualities, it is sent in bags of 10 or 12 stones, of 16 lbs. each, to be teased, which may be considered the first process in the manufacture! the workman then spreads a layer of wool on the factory floor, and over this wool he sprinkles, by means of a can of a peculiar construction, a quantity of whale oil, (generally in the proportion of one quart per stone,) exactly in the same manner as a gardener watering his plants. Upon this he spreads another layer of wool, oiling it as before, and so on, till the whole is done. This oiling process overcomes in part the ruffness of the fibres, and enables them to slide more easily among each other in carding and spinning. It will be easily seen, that the oil will be pretty equally distributed among the wool, in the act of teasing, where it remains till the wool is formed into cloth: the cloth is then sent to the fulling mill, to have the oil washed and cleaned out by means of urine, fuller's-earth, and water.

Now, as it is imposible for any one to handle a soot bag

without getting begrimed with the soot, so it is equally clear, that wool thus all but saturated with oil, will soil not only the hands, face, and clothes of the work-people, but the machines, walls, and floor of the factory, (I have seen it dripping through the floors,) or anything which comes in contact with it, and also emits a very unpleasant odour.

Another source of the offensive smell arises from the quantity of oil used in oiling the machinery. People who are at all acquainted with machinery, well know, that shafts, wheels, and spindles, in short anything, even a common wheel-barrow, that revolves upon its axis, requires to be kept clean and well oiled, in order that it may revolve smoothly and silently, and to prevent the undue friction or wearing of the brass step or collar in which it moves. For spindles and other light machinery oiling is sufficient; but for heavy pieces, such as upright, horizontal, and cylinder shafts, oil alone would not do, unless it was constantly dripping upon the part; and as that would be very expensive, the following cheap substitute is applied.

The fat of horses, dogs, pigs, and many other animals, which die a natural death, or are killed with some incurable disease upon them, is sold to the manufacturers, and kept for the purpose of greasing the heavy machinery. It may be imagined what sort of an effluvia will arise from the application of this fat to shafts almost on fire. I have frequently been sent to order this article, and have had to apply it to a shaft very much heated, and as one piece melted away, another was laid on till it got cooled, and all the time the smoke was arising almost sufficient to suffocate me.

One great cause of ill health to the operatives in factories, is the dust and lime which is continually flying about. A large quantity of skin-wool and cow's-hair are used in the manufacture of coarse rugs, carpets, &c. This is obtained from the skins of the animals after they are killed, by means of a strong solution of lime-water. This lime thus gets intermixed with the wool and hair, and in this state it is sold to the manufacturer; it is then put through the teaser, in order to shake out the lime and dust; and, as the teaser goes at an immense speed, the work-people, the machine, and all around, are covered with the lime; and consequently, every inspiration of air in such an atmosphere, must carry with it and lodge upon the lungs a portion of these pernicious ingredients: the result is, difficulty of breathing, asthma, &c.

On finding myself settled for life in the factories, as it was then pretty evident I should not be able to do anything else, I began to think of getting a step higher in the works. It will be necessary to observe, that hitherto I had only been a piecer; so I put myself forward as well as I was able, and master soon noticed me, and gave me a higher place, where the labour was not so very distressing, but the care and responsibility was greater; and although I was a complete cripple, I now began to feel a little more comfortable.

A great many are made cripples by over-exertion. Among those who have been brought up from infancy with me in the factories, and whom death has spared, few have escaped without some injury. My brother-in-law and myself have been crippled by this cause, but in different ways; my sister partly by over-exertion and partly by machinery. On going home to breakfast one morning, I was much surprised at seeing several of the neighbours and two doctors in our house. On inquiring the cause, I found that my second sister had nearly lost her hand in the machinery. She had been working all night, and, fatigued and sleepy, had not been so watchful as she otherwise would have been; and consequently, her right hand became entangled in the machine which she was attending. Four iron teeth of a wheel, three-quarters of an inch broad, and one-quarter of an inch thick, had been forced through her hand, from the back part, among the leaders, &c.; and the fifth iron tooth fell upon the thumb, and crushed it to atoms. It was thought, for some time, that she would lose her hand. But it was saved; and, as you may be sure, it is stiff and contracted, and is but a very feeble apology for a hand. This accident might have been prevented, if the wheels above referred to had been boxed off, which they might have been for a couple of shillings ; and the very next week after this accident, a man had two fingers taken off his hand, by the very same wheels—and still they are not boxed off!

The gentlemen she was working for at the time had immense wealth, most of which, I have reason to believe, was got by the factories. They paid the doctor, and gave her ten shillings !—which was about three farthings per day for the time she was off work. To this sum was added seven shillings more, subscribed by the work-people ! I need not say, that she has been a cripple ever since, and can do very little towards getting a living.

After the wool has been oiled, as before described, it is then put through the first teaser,* from which it is carried to the second teaser,† where it is prepared for the carding-

---

* The first teaser is a machine for breaking up the fleece wool, and consists of a very strong, firmly made cylinder, about 5 feet diameter, and 3 feet broad. Into the surface of this cylinder are firmly screwed a large quantity of iron spikes, about the size of a man's finger, in diagonal lines, about 2 or 3 inches apart from each other: in front of this cylinder are 2 rollers, called feeding rollers, about 8 inches in diameter, also filled with teeth of a different description. These rollers work into each other in such a manner as to hold the fleece of wool firmly between them, and as they revolve but slowly, they present the wool gradually to the teeth of the cylinder, which performs 400 or 500 revolutions per minute. The momentum of this cylinder in motion is very great, and the wool or anything which comes in its way is torn in pieces, and thrown out behind. When it is going at full speed, the machine, the floor, and everything around, are in a constant shake. It is called among the work-people the Devil, from its tearing off the arms, &c. of the workmen. I have known 3 arms torn off, and 2 lives lost in consequence, in my time ; and I must allow, that I have felt timid, when working at the very same machine that had a little while before been so employed.

† The second teaser is a more complicated machine than the first: it consists of a large cylinder and a number of rollers filled with teeth made of iron or steel, of the size and shape of a cock's spur, and thence called "cock-spurs." This teaser opens the wool more equally, and prepares it for the carding-engine : its capabilities of doing mischief to the work-people is nearly equal to that of the first teaser.

c

engine. I had once a very narrow escape from death by this machine, when about 16 years of age, in the following manner :—

After finishing one sort of wool, it is usual to clean all the loose wool from the top and sides of the machine, previous to beginning another sort. This I was doing in the usual way, with a broom, and, as use begets habits of carelessness in boys, I had not used that degree of care requisite in such places. The consequence was, that the cylinder of the machine caught hold of the broom, and, if I had not had the presence of mind to let go my hold, I must have been dragged in with it. The broom was torn in a thousand pieces—a great number of the iron teeth were broken out and scattered in all directions—and, by the care of a kind Providence, I came off with a few slight wounds, from these teeth having stuck into me in several places.

The wool is then handed forward from the second teaser to the carding-engine*, where it is prepared for the piecer; it was in this sort of engine my sister had her right hand so dreadfully lacerated.

When about 15 years of age, a circumstance occurred to me which does not often fall to the lot of factory children, and which had a great influence on my future life. I happened one day to find an old board laying useless in a corner of the factory. On this board, with a piece of chalk, I was scrawling out, as well as I was able, the initials of my name, instead of attending to my work, as I ought to have been doing. Having formed the letters W. D., I was laying down the board, and turning to my work, when, judge of my surprise, at perceiving one of my masters looking over my shoulder. Of course, I expected a scolding; but the half

* The carding-engine may be briefly described as composed of 3 cylinders, from 4 to 5 feet diameter, 3 other cylinders, from 2 to 3 feet diameter, and from 20 to 30 rollers of different dimensions, all covered with cards. The wool is spread very equally upon cloths which carry it to the first cylinder, by which it is taken forward to the second, and so on till it comes out at the other end, in cardings ready for the piecer.

smile upon his countenance suddenly dispelled my fears. He kindly asked me several questions about my writing and reading, and, after gently chiding me for taking improper opportunities, he gave me two-pence to purchase paper, pens, and ink—which sum he continued weekly for several years, always inspecting my humble endeavours, and suggesting any improvements which he thought necessary. He also (with the approbation of his brother, the other partner in the firm,) allowed me to leave work an hour earlier than the other work-people every evening for a whole winter, in order that I might improve myself; and thus an opportunity was afforded me, which, with a few presents of books, &c. from both masters, were the means, under Providence, of laying the foundation of what I now consider a tolerable education.

This kindness on the part of my masters will never be erased from my memory. It is as fresh to me now as if it had occurred but yesterday.

With this encouragement, and impelled by the activity of my own mind, and an irresistible thirst after knowledge, I set myself earnestly to the acquisition of such branches of education as I thought might better my condition in after-life; and, although I had still my work to attend, I soon had the happiness to find myself in possession of a tolerable share of mathematics, geography, history, and several branches of natural and experimental philosophy.

So long as I was pursuing these studies, the thoughts of my unhappy condition were in some measure assuaged. But, in proportion as the truths of science were unfolded to my wondering sight, and the mists of ignorance chased from my mind, so the horrors of my situation became daily more and more apparent, and made me, if possible, still more fretful and unhappy! It was evident to me, that I was intended for a nobler purpose than to be a factory slave! and I longed for an opportunity to burst the trammels by which I was kept in bondage!

Being desirous of turning my newly-acquired learning to some account, I engaged with a tailor, a neighbour of ours, to keep his books, draw out his bills, &c., in the evenings; by which means, I earned part of my clothing, and also got an insight into the trade, which was of service to me afterwards.

I became acquainted with a young man, who was very kind in lending me books, and explaining any difficulty I might be labouring under in my studies. I shall never forget his kindness;—he was to me like a brother. And now that I began to derive pleasure from the perusal of books, (and, in fact, it was the only source of pleasure I had) I did not omit any opportunity of gratifying it, particularly on the Sabbath day. It was customary for me, in the summer months, to take a book, and a crust of bread in my pocket, on a Sunday morning, and go to a very retired and secluded wood, about two miles from the town of Kendal, in which I lived, and there I spent the day alone, on the banks of a rivulet that ran through the wood. I have sat for hours together absorbed in study, unperceived by mortal eye, with nothing to disturb me, but the numerous little songsters that kept up a continual concert, as if to make the place still more enchanting to my imagination. These were seasons of real pleasure to me; they were also attended with some advantages in other respects.

I had for many years enjoyed but a delicate state of health, owing to constant confinement, the smells of the factory, &c.; but these Sunday excursions got me a better appetite for my victuals, and I became more healthy and strong. I also derived considerable pleasure and improvement from the study of nature, in watching the habits of birds, bees, ants, butterflies, and, in short, any natural curiosity that came in my way; and when the evenings began to close in around me, and compelled me to return to the habitations of men, I felt a reluctance to leave my quiet and solitary retreat.

On some occasions, when I have been returning from my retreat in the wood on a Sunday evening, I have stood upon an eminence at a distance, and watched the gaily-attired inhabitants taking their evening walk in the fields and meadows around the town, and could not help contrasting their situation with mine. They were happy in themselves, anxious to see and be seen, and deriving pleasure from mutual friendship and intercourse: I, with the seeds of misery implanted in my nature, surrounded by circumstances calculated to make me truly unhappy,—shrinking from the face of men to a lonely wood, to brood over my sorrows in secret and in silence. They were enjoying the fruits of their industry, but the reward of mine was—misery, wretchedness, and disease.

On one occasion, I was tempted to have recourse to a little of what the world calls policy, in order to gratify my appetite for reading, and which I knew at the time to be wrong. It was usual for us to stop the mill on the Saturday evening at five o'clock; then, after cleaning myself, I had a few hours to call my own, which were generally spent in my favourite occupation. One fine Saturday evening in June, I took a walk to the ruins of an old castle which overlooks the town of Kendal, and which was to me a very agreeable retreat from the noise and bustle of the factory, having previously laid out the only two-pence I had in the loan of a book, which I had got snugly in my pocket, and was calculating on the pleasure it would afford me during the week. It chanced, however, to be one of those thinly printed volumes with large margins; and seating myself on the above-mentioned ruins, I did not rise till I had finished it: when I did, the grey of the evening was fast closing in around me. But I had exhausted my whole week's stock of amusement. What was to be done? I could not think of borrowing two-pence for another volume, because I had no means of paying it back again. At last I hit upon a plan, which, after a little hesitation, I carried into effect. I took the volume back to the librarian, and requested him to change it for another, telling him it did not suit me. He, being a good-natured sort of man, did so, little thinking that I had read it through. I felt ashamed, and for a long time after could scarcely look in the man's face, but I made it up to him in another way, when I had it in my power.

But having completed my second seven years of servitude, (somewhat earlier, indeed, than it is usual for workmen to have finished their first,) I got advanced to 9s. per week, and began to think myself well to do in the world, and could, by following a rigid course of economy, spare a shilling or two occasionally for the purchase of such books as I took a fancy to. I kept an account of every item of expenditure, and regularly balanced up once a month; and, though it may surprise many, my expenses for board, lodging, and washing, over a space of three years, averaged exactly 7s. per week; so that I had 2s. a week left for clothes and books; and being a member of the Mechanics' Institute, I became acquainted with the librarian, who engaged me to assist him in giving out books two evenings in the week, which added a little to my resources.

When I came to that period of life when men generally think of taking a partner, and settling in some way in the world, I was again beset by insurmountable obstacles. I saw my more fortunate fellow workmen getting married, and settling around me—I saw them comfortable and happy in their families, and I almost envied them their happiness. But no remedy was at hand: to have married a factory girl, would only have involved both myself and her in greater troubles, I being a cripple; and it would have been something remarkable, if I could have met with one able to make a shirt. How could it be expected from those who had been so wretchedly treated?—who were sent into this world to be the comfort and solace of man, and who, had their faculties been allowed to develope under a more genial sun, might have been the pride and ornament of the age in which they lived. But how different is the sad reality! They have been kept as slaves at one toilsome task, till every fine feeling of their nature is blunted. Ignorant of everything calculated to elevate and raise them to that high station originally intended for them by their Creator, is it to be wondered at, if we find them sunk, degraded, and almost lost to every sense of shame?* and for me to have looked for a partner in another class of society, situated as I then was, would have been ridiculous in the extreme.

To turn my thoughts from my pitiful situation, I attended lectures on various subjects, repeated the simple experiments at home, made some curious models and drawings of machines, and could thus contrive to pass away my leisure time pleasantly. Besides, one of my sisters dying, left a son; and her husband being unable to provide for him, it was a source of pleasure and gratification for me to attend to his wants and improvement.

Although I was not, at this time, constantly employed within the mills, but had to attend to the packing department in the warehouse, and any other place about the works where I might be required, yet still the effects of former years of factory toil were on me — still my life was one of suffering, although not to so great a degree; and having it now in my power to procure comforts which before were unknown to me, I lived something more like a Christian than I had formerly been enabled to do.

Thinking I might stand in need of assistance at some future period of my life, as I had all along been obliged to prop myself up, and was evidently working above my strength, I joined the Society of Odd Fellows, which is the best of this description that I am acquainted with; but it is not without its faults. In this Society I was soon put into office; and, having an active and persevering mind, I put myself forward, and was elected as the Secretary of the Lodge to which I belonged. On that occasion, I well remember, I had to address, for the first time in my life, a

---

* I have seen some young women brought to work in the factories, who had been nurses in respectable families, and who seemed to be shocked, on their introduction, with what they heard and saw; but a very short time in such a school made them as bad as the rest.

large body of men. I felt rather timid; but having prac-
tised in my room for a full hour, I delivered my maiden
speech, which still remains fixed on my memory, as follows:

" Mr. Chairman and Gentlemen,—I now stand before you
as a candidate for the important office of Secretary—an
office which, I am well aware, requires not only talent and
abilities, but also great care and attention—(hear, hear);
and although I can say nothing in favour of my humble
abilities, having received no other education than what I
have been able to scrape together after my day's work was
done, still I trust that the interest I feel for the good and
welfare of this Society, will stimulate me to use every exer-
tion in my power in the discharge of the several duties of
this office, should I be thought worthy of holding it. As I
am convinced that you will act in this, as in all other matters, solely for the good of the Society, so I can assure you,
that I shall be satisfied with your decision, whether it be
for or against me."

There were five candidates for the office; and this was
the state of the poll, as taken from the minute-book :—

William Dodd 64
W. S. 4
J. D.......................... 4
J. B. 4
J. M. 4
————
80

The other candidates thought I should have the lead,
but each expressed a wish to be second. The result proved
they were all second. These four members were trades-
men's sons, who had received a good education—I a factory
cripple, who had never cost my parents a shilling for my
learning. I was elected a second time to this office, and
had, in 12 months, about 300*l.* of the Society's money
through my fingers. I then received a vote of thanks, and
was elected to a higher office. In the year 1835, I was
elected to represent the district, a body of 700 men, in the

annual meeting of the Society held that year at Derby; and in 1836 I was again thought worthy of a seat in that important meeting held in London. I shall have to speak of this Society again.

An easy clerk's situation being now vacant, I was advised by some friends to avail myself of the opportunity, and thus free myself totally from the factories, especially as I had several influential friends to forward my views. I mentioned the subject to my masters, and, after considering it, they made such advantageous offers, as induced me to remain with them. This step I shall have reason to regret as long as I live.

In 1834, the present law for the regulation of factories was about being put in force. I, being appointed timekeeper for the works, had to take the children before the doctor to be examined, as certificates were required from him, that they were of proper age to be admitted into the factory. I cannot describe my feelings as I went on those occasions, accompanied by about a score of little stunted figures, some of whom had been working in the factories for years, and whose parents had been in vain trying to get them something else to do; but I well remember, that I had great difficulty in convincing the doctor of their being of the age required, although I had no doubt of it myself, as I was well acquainted with their parents at the time of the children's birth; but their appearance was so much against them, that I fancied on some occasions, from certain expressions that the doctor made use of, that he thought I was deceiving him. Had he known my inmost thoughts, he would not for a moment have suspected me.

One of the most trying circumstances that occurred to me in all my factory experience, happened in the winter of 1834-5. I had then a youth, of about 17 years of age, placed under me, for the purpose of learning some of the higher branches of the business. I had been giving him directions what to do one day, and had gone up into the room above, for the purpose of superintending some other part of the works, when suddenly one branch of the machinery stopped, and, on turning round to inquire the cause, I was met by several persons, nearly out of breath, who said to me, " Tom has got into the gig, and is killed." I ran down in haste, but it was too true : he was strangled. A great many bones were broken, and several ghastly wounds were inflicted on various parts of his person !

After his mangled body was extracted from the machinery, by unscrewing and taking the machine in pieces, it was laid in a recess on the ground-floor, the same in which the accident occurred, to await a coroner's inquest, the works being all stopped, and the hands dismissed. One by one they gradually went home, and left me alone for some time. The reader may more easily imagine, than I can describe my feelings on this occasion, as I paced, with folded arms, the flags of this dreary place. It was a cold, wet night. I had a flickering light burning beside me, just sufficient to cast a sombre and gloomy appearance over the three water-wheels and the heavy machinery by which I was surrounded. Not a sound broke upon my ear, except the wind and rain without, and the water trickling through the wheels within, with the mangled remains of that youth, whom I had carefully instructed in his business, and looked upon almost like a son, laying bleeding beside me.

This boy's death occurred partly through his own carelessness, as he had no business at the place; but the same thing might have happened to people who had business there; and consequently, it shows the necessity of boxing up all parts of machines, and the gearing by which such machines are propelled, where there is the least appearance of danger. Had this precaution been adopted in every mill, such calamities could not have happened; and, in many thousands of cases, limbs and lives which have been lost would have been preserved.

If anything was wanted to make me disgusted with the system, this and other circumstances would have supplied the deficiency; for while I and hundreds of work-people were toiling and sweating day after day for the bare necessaries of life—struggling, as it were, against wind and tide, and still hoping that some favourable turn would afford a resting-place for our wearied and emaciated frames—the manufacturers were amassing immense wealth, and thus converting what ought to have been a national blessing into a national curse—" adding field to field, and house to house," and rolling about in their carriages, surrounded by every luxury that this world can give, and looking upon us poor factory slaves as if we had been a different race of beings, created only to be worked to death for their gain.

As there is various reports respecting the wages of factory labourers, I here subjoin a table of the money received by me from 1810 to the close of my factory experience:—

Age.		Weekly Wages.						Yearly Amount.		
		s.	d.	s.	d.	s.	d.	£.	s.	d.
6 to	7*	1	0..1		3..1		6	2	5	0
7	8			1	6..1		9	4	4	6
8	9					2	3	5	17	0
9	10					2	6	6	10	0
10	11					2	6	6	10	0
11	12					2	8	6	18	8
12	13					2	10	7	7	4
13	14					3	0	7	16	0
14	15					3	6	9	2	0
15	16					4	0	10	8	0
16	17					5	0	13	0	0
17	18					6	0	15	12	0
18	19					7	0	18	4	0
19	20					8	0	20	16	0
20	21					9	0	23	8	0
21	22					10	0	26	0	0
22	23					11	0	28	12	0
23	24					11	0	28	12	0
24	25					12	0	31	4	0
25	26					12	0	31	4	0
26	27					13	6	35	2	0
27	28					13	6	35	2	0
28	29					15	0	39	0	0
29	30					15	0	39	0	0
30	31					17	0	44	4	0
31	32					17	0	44	4	0
Done up								540	2	6
* Part of this year was occupied in card making.		Overtime - -						9	17	6
								550	0	0
		Average about			8		3			

It cannot, with truth or justice, be said that I was an idle workman, or an indifferent hand at my business. I have documents from my master to prove that I was not idle; and the fact of my having been selected from a number of workmen to attend improved and expensive machinery for finishing cloths, with which machinery I was doing as much work as six men by hand, and where I was obliged to lock myself in the room alone, and not allow any one to enter but my master, and sometimes an assistant, (in this manner I have worked for many years,) affords a sufficient proof that I thoroughly understood my business. Besides, the latter part of my time I was a confidential servant, and in this capacity had to receive and pay money, occasionally attending the post office and bank with letters, bills, &c., and have had frequently upwards of 1,000*l.* passing through my hands in a week. At this time I was receiving 3*s.* or 4*s.* a week more than many strong, able-bodied men, which would not have been the case, if I had not been considered worthy of it. This will at once prove that I was receiving as much, or more, than the generality of workmen; and that this table is by no means to be considered an under rate of wages. It is, at least, 70*l.* or 80*l.* more than my brother-in-law has received in the same time.

From the first day I went into the factories, till the time that I left, my lost time, in sickness, holidays, &c., amounted to about four months. This lost time I have worked up at least three times over. When we were busy, I have worked as many as 18 hours per day; and yet all I have received, whether as wages, over-time, perquisites, &c., does not amount, as the preceding table will show, to more than 550*l.*; and for this paltry sum I have sacrificed my health, strength, constitution, nay, almost life itself; while those who have been reaping the benefit of my labours, have been laying by their thousands yearly and every year, and are now wallowing in riches, but nothing awaits me except the workhouse.

Let us see, on the other hand, what would have been the

result, had I been brought up to a trade—say a carpenter and joiner, for instance. In that case I should have contracted a considerable debt before I began to receive any benefit—say 50*l.*, for apprentice fee, tools, and clothes, the master finding, as is usual, meat and lodging: then, at 21 years of age, it is reasonable to suppose I should have been a free man, with a good robust form and constitution; and supposing I had earned 1*l.* per week for 20 years, 15*s.* per week for 10 years, and 12*s.* per week for 9 years more, (which, I think, is a reasonable estimate,) this would have brought me to 60 years of age, beyond which no man, in my opinion, ought to work. At this rate, I should have earned, as a journeyman, 1,710*l.* 16*s.*; then, deducting 160*l.* 16*s.* for the repayment of apprentice fee, tools, and any other incidental expenses, it would leave 1,550*l.*, which is 1,000*l.* more than I have earned in the factories; and, instead of being subject to daily and excruciating pains, I might have passed through life in comparative comfort, might with confidence have encountered the expenses of a wife and family, enjoyed the evening of my days surrounded by a smiling offspring, and sunk into the grave at peace with myself and all the world. But how different is the picture of my sad fate!

The way in which the bones in the legs become distorted, I mentioned in a former page: I shall here say a few words upon the shapes they assume. The most common is that of in-kneed cripples, generally the right knee, sometimes the left, frequently both, as my own. In this case, when standing in the easiest position, the feet are about 14 inches apart, the knees and thighs are then pressing close together, so that the legs form a sort of arch for the support of the body. On taking a side view of a person standing so, he appears in the act of kneeling, about half way down; the outsides of the feet or abutments of the arch are flat and burst open the shoes, the centre of gravity crossing the thigh and leg bones. Another shape is that furnished by an acquaintance of mine, of the name of Hutton, near Bradford, in Yorkshire, whom I met with in London, a short time ago, and who was put into the factories about the same time as myself, perfectly straight and strong. This man's legs are both turned one way—the right knee in, and the left knee out; so that the legs and thighs are parallel throughout, but forming an angle of about 60 degrees. He is almost frightful to look upon. A brother of his, who was also straight on entering, is still worse. His legs are curved *both outwards*, so that a person may run a wheel-barrow between them. These are some of the most common shapes, but there are others equally bad.

One evil arising from the bending and curving of the legs is the state of the blood-vessels; for if the bones go wrong, the blood-vessels must go wrong also. Nature has provided a beautiful contrivance for propelling the blood to every part of the human frame. This is done, in a well-formed person, with perfect ease, without any appearance of difficulty whatever. But it is not so with us factory cripples. Our blood lodges, as it were, in little pools, in crannies and corners; and the apparatus for forcing it along, instead of being stronger, as in our case required, it is actually weaker, in consequence of our weak state of body. Thus, our very life, (for life depends upon the circulation of the blood,) at best, is only like the half-extinguished flame of a gas-burner, when there is water in the pipes—it jumps and flickers for a little while, and then pops out. But in order to keep it even in this state, we are obliged to have recourse to friction daily, and every day.

One serious evil resulting from this imperfect circulation of the blood, is the drying up of the marrow in the bones. The bones then decay, as in my arm; amputation is resorted to, or life is lost.

A variety of shapes is also visible in the curvature of the spine of factory cripples.

With respect to cripples who have been made so by over-exertion, it is usual for manufacturers to throw the blame entirely upon the parents of such children. How they can divest themselves of all blame, appears to me parodoxical. I cannot look upon them in any other light than as accessaries to the mischief, especially when it is considered that the several cases of distortion of the spine, contraction and other deformities of the limbs, &c., did not take place all in a minute, but that they were coming gradually on for years, and immediately under the eye of the manufacturers, who, by a single word, might have dismissed them from the place, and thus have saved them from utter ruin.

There are a great variety of cripples made by machinery. The most common are those wanting arms and legs, or whose arms and legs have been crushed or torn, and rendered useless.

A fine young girl is now laying under the hands of the doctor, from an accident in the same mill as my sister had her hand torn in. She, poor girl, has had *her leg torn off*, *both her thigh-bones broken*, and also received several internal and external injuries. Accidents by machinery in the North are of weekly, nay, almost daily occcrrence.

A list of physicians cases would be too long for me to furnish here.

Looking over, in my mind's eye, those boys and girls who were employed in the factories when I commenced, and who, like me, have been kept close to it from their youth upwards, I find they are generally weak, stunted, and in many cases deformed in person, childish, and ignorant in mind, not having been accustomed to some of the most important duties of life, (their whole faculties have been absorbed in the daily routine of factory labour,) they make, as it is very natural to suppose, but " sorry " heads of families; and their children, as a matter of course, are compelled, by dire necessity, to pass through the same dull, tedious, miserable state of existence.

Spinners suffer considerably. Some of my former masters have died, with every symptom of premature old age upon them, at 45 to 50. The overlooker has no very enviable birth. He has to study the interest of the master, the men, and his own. His own is usually consulted by having a general shop, where the work-people can lay out their money, and by lending small sums, with the understanding to receive interest after the modest rate of 65 per centum per annum, which I have paid. Yet some of them deserve all they get: they are generally ill-paid for their harassing duties. The baneful influence of the system extends even to the manufacturers themselves. As an instance, I may mention the case of the kind master who encouraged me to read and write, and whom, from long service, I looked upon with as much respect and love as if he had been my father. On some occasions when I have been in the counting-house with him, and especially after an unsuccessful journey — when some other manufacturer has been selling goods cheaper than he was—I have fancied I could see the canker-worm, care, corroding and eating into his very existence. The last time I had an opportunity of seeing this gentleman was on the 19th of May, 1840, in St. Martin's-le-Grand. He was with another gentleman, who I took, in the distance, to be his brother. I was on my way to the hospital, with my arm in a sling—that arm I was so soon to lose. He was an exception to the general character of the manufacturers. He died shortly after; and it is my opinion, that had he not been connected with the factories, he might have protracted his existence to a later date.

About two or three years before I left the factories, my mother being then on her death-bed, I thought it was time to look about me for a partner; and being then in comfortable circumstances, on good terms with my master, and everything appearing fair, I almost forgot I was a cripple, and began to look about me for a steady servant girl, on whom I could depend. I had no difficulty in finding one to my mind, and occasionally accompanied her to church and other places. People began to pass remarks; and even my masters spoke of my being about to marry, and were divided in opinion. One said he thought I should not, considering the state I was in — the other said I might do very well.

However, the girl was too wise to join her destinies with those of a factory cripple. She left the town, and refused to answer my letters, which was a sufficient reason for my discontinuing to write.

Then I got acquainted with another respectable girl. She also soon left the town, but continued to correspond with me for some time, without signing her name. She soon broke off.

So I thought that I would go to work in another way; and in order to afford a convincing proof that I really did wish to get married, I took a house, and had it well furnished. I then laid siege to a third, and made myself quite sure — there could be no mistake about the matter this time: and as I had heard that after a certain age women would take up with anything, I thought I would try one older than myself. So I paid my addresses to a respectable housekeeper, who had known me for years, and who, apparently, was pleased with my attentions. She would walk with me to church, to a place of amusement, to her relations to take tea, in the fields, or anywhere but to the trap that I had baited for her. So I began to think old birds were not to be caught with chaff. However, I did not like the idea of giving up to be laughed at, so I persevered, and pressed my suit more warmly, but soon found that she was only playing with me, like a cat with a mouse.

One evening, being almost driven to desperation, I went with a determination to have a final answer before we parted. I got half way to her place of residence, and was about to return, in consequence of the moon at that time shining out, and showing my figure before me. However, I went into a public-house, had a glass of ale, and, thus inspired, went on again. When I got there, I was kindly received, as usual; so I made my business known as well as I could, and gave her to understand that I was determined to have an answer. She patiently heard all I had got to say; and I watched every muscle of her countenance, as if

E

my very existence had depended upon her answer. I saw a slight curl of the upper lip—her eyes then began to descend, till they settled the intensity of their gaze upon my knees. At that moment, I wished the earth to open and swallow me up. She, seeing me agitated, took compassion, and told me, what she might have told me at the first, she declined. Thus was I compelled either to return and take a factory girl, (any of whom would have thought themselves highly honoured by the offer,) or live and die a bachelor. I chose the latter as the most preferable.

I have done everything that laid in my power to prevent the evils that have come upon me, and to avert the consequences of those evils I could not prevent, by endeavouring to transplant myself into a more genial soil; but all my exertions have proved fruitless. Wherever I turned for succour, wherever I looked for sympathy or kindly feeling, I was met by repulses, derision, and insult; and this because I was a factory cripple, and aspired to associate with those whom I considered in a more respectable sphere of life. The best feelings of my heart were played with, wounded, crushed, and trampled on; and ultimately, I was driven back, like the daw in the fable, stripped of every feather, to the miserable squad from which I attempted to emigrate, there to encounter the sneers and the buffets of my fellow slaves.

Having now resolved to lead a bachelor's life, for the best of all reasons, not being able to avoid it, I contrived many little helps to make myself as comfortable as I could. I got some self-acting cooking utensils, by means of which I was able to get a warm dinner at the expense of one farthing. So long as the fine warm weather lasted, this Robinson Crusoe sort of life did very well; but when winter came, and I had no fire to go to, and very often wet and cold, it was too much for me to bear. Besides, I had not been able entirely to forget my fair teaser; and giving way under the difficulty, I tried to drown my cares in drink. This only made bad worse, and got me into errors, besides wasting my money; so I resolved to give up my house, sell my furniture, and go to lodgings: and thus terminated my fruitless endeavour to get married.

I now turned my attention again to getting totally away from the factories; and getting acquainted with Mr. Hill, schoolmaster of the British and Foreign School in Kendal, and being informed by that gentleman of the advantages held out to young men by the Society in the Borough Road to become teachers, I was inclined to think it might suit me to come and be instructed. This gentleman kindly undertook to apply for me, describing minutely my person. He received for answer, they were sorry to inform him, that in consequence of being a cripple, I could not be admitted. I applied to other schools in the same way, and received the same answer. My masters, partly to encourage me, established a night school for the piecers, and I attended two evenings in the week, and thus drilled myself into teaching. I had a twelvemonth's practice in this way. We could scarcely keep the piecers awake, they were so done up. Sometimes they would fall off the form on to the floor, quite overcome with sleep.

Being weary of the factories, and having prepared myself, as well as I was able, I opened a school in the early part of the year 1837, for the instruction of youth in reading, writing, and arithmetic; in hopes by this means to avert the impending danger that had so long threatened me. But I had not been in it long before the school-room was wanted by the proprietor, and, not meeting with another to suit me, I came up to London to the annual meeting of Odd Fellows, as before mentioned.

While in London, I thought I would try to procure a situation as clerk, and was encouraged in this idea by a distant relation, a licensed victualler, who kindly offered to take me into his bar till I succeeded in my wish. I accepted the offer. A few months after, an opportunity presented itself. It being necessary to write to my old masters for a character, I did so, and received the following answer :—

"Kendal, 10 mo., 6th, 1837.

"William Dodd, to whom we direct this, was in our
employ for many years, and during that time was a trust-
worthy servant. We can give him a good character for
sobriety and industry. He was in our employ as a ware-
houseman and packer, with some attention to the books.
"ISAAC AND WILLIAM WILSON."

"P.S.—W. D. left our situation about nine months ago."

The gentleman I was with, as barman, took a liking to
me, and wanted to retain me in his service; but it being a
line of life unsuitable for me, I was anxious to leave it as
soon as possible, but not having any friend in London but
him, I did not like to leave contrary to his wish. In his house
I remained nearly 12 months, when I was taken ill, and had
to go to Gravesend for the benefit of my health; and after
five weeks' absence I again returned, and was in his service
seven months longer. He then sold off part of his business,
and had no more occasion for my services, but kindly allowed
me to stay with him a few weeks; and as nobody would
give me any work to do, I resolved to go into the west and
south of England to seek employment. But very little employment was then to be met with for able-bodied men; as
for cripples it was out of the question. Thus I travelled some
hundreds of miles, sometimes riding a little, but generally
walking: I also crossed over to the Isle of Wight, and visited
all the places likely to afford me any employment, and could
have got work if I had been a tailor or shoemaker, but not
being either, and no chance of anything else turning up, I
retraced my steps to London, having paid the last two-pence
I had in the world to the boatman at Portsmouth.

While I was in the public line in London, I had to deal
with all sorts of people, from the lowest to the highest. I
heard all sorts of coarse brutal expressions; but in all that
time, I never heard anything more vulgar, brutal, or wicked,
than I was accustomed to hear from the master-manufac-
turers, in my younger days—from men too who had received

a liberal education, and who were called to fill the highest office in the town, and who, from their superior station in life, ought to have set an example worthy of imitating. The men eagerly followed the example set them by the masters, and cursing, swearing, and low language became the order of the day. Respecting the moral conduct of the young, I can say but little; any one may think for himself what will be the result of 100 young people of both sexes working together under such circumstances, going together in the morning, associating with each other through the day, and returning again in the evening with no moral restraint upon their action, no pattern shewn them worthy of imitating; and where acts of gross indecency, low, vulgar, brutal language, singing immoral songs, swearing, &c. are not only tolerated, but in many instances, actually countenanced and encouraged. A person brought up from infancy to maturity in such a school, and who can then retire with clean hands, or a clear conscience, must possess something more in his composition than human nature can boast of—must be such an one as I never yet met with, such an one as I am sure does not exist.*

In my travels through the country in search of employment, I had frequent opportunity of witnessing the condition of the labourers in agricultural districts, I conversed with many who received only 8s. or 9s. per week as wages, who were surrounded by more real comforts than many of my class with several shillings per week more. This may be accounted for by the fact that 8s. in the hands of an agricultural labourer, is at all times equal to 10s. or 11s. in the hands of a manufacturing labourer: and this does not arise from any carelessness or extravagance on the part of the latter. For instance, an agricultural labourer enjoys many privileges and advantages that the other knows nothing of —such as an allowance of potatoes, turnips, and other vege-

---

* The scenes which I have witnessed, and it is with sorrow I say have in some instances been participater in, are of such a nature, as to be improper to lay before the public eye.

tables, and in many cases wood for the fire; his rent is also considerably lower; he also enjoys the blessings of breathing the pure air. Now, the manufacturing labourer cannot eat his machines or anything he may be making; and in consequence of inhaling the pernicious ingredients from the atmosphere in which he moves, and the nauseous smells by which he is surrounded, he cannot eat his food with a relish, and he is occasionally obliged to have recourse to medicine; and should he have any cripples in the family, (which is generally the case,) he must have a supply of flannel and linen bandages, oils, drugs, &c. constantly by him; and these little things form a considerable item in his expenditure. In all my experience, I do not remember ever to have been three months at one time free from bandages; and I have worked for weeks together with three or four of my joints thus secured.

The behaviour of agricultural labourers and their children is much superior to anything we meet with in manufacturing towns; and I have no doubt many of my readers will have noticed this in travelling through the country. This is easily accounted for. They are surrounded by circumstances so totally different, that there is no wonder at it. In the first place, the society around them is more polished and enlightened: in their daily toil they meet with so many instances of the wisdom and power of an all-wise being, that a love for his handiworks is sure to be impressed upon their mind;—the cheering influence of the sun, the refreshing breeze, the singing of birds, &c., all inspire this feeling. The manufacturing labourer knows nothing of these blessings by experience. He is placed in a mill or factory as a machine, for the performance of a quantity of labour— he hears nothing but the rumbling noise of the machinery, or the harsh voice of the overlooker—sees nothing but an endless variety of shafts, drums, straps, and wheels in motion; and though these may, at first, inspire him with a feeling of respect for, and admiration of, the inventive powers of his fellow-creatures, yet this feeling will vanish, when he reflects on their power to destroy or render useless for life that exalted piece of mechanism formed by and after the image of God!

I was forcibly struck with the kind behaviour of the agricultural labourers to me. The manner in which the family generally met together in the evening, brought to my mind the following beautiful description of a cottager's Saturday night, by Burns:—

" At length his lonely cot appears in view,
    Beneath the shelter of an aged tree;
  Th' expectant *wee-things*, toddlin, stacher through
    To meet their Dad, wi' flichterin noise and glee.
  His wee-bit ingle, blinkin bonnilie,
    His clean hearthstane, his thrifty *wifie's* smile,
  The lisping infant prattling on his knee,
    Does a' his weary carking cares beguile,
  And makes him quite forget his labour and his toil.

" Belyve the elder bairns come drapping in,
    At service out amang the farmers roun';
  Some ca' the pleugh, some herd, some tentie rin
    A cannie errand to a neebor town;
  Their eldest hope, their *Jenny*, woman grown,
    In youthfu' bloom, love sparklin in her ee,
  Comes hame, perhaps, to show a braw new gown,
    Or deposite her sair-won penny fee,
  To help her parents dear, if they in hardship be.

" Wi' joy unfeign'd brothers and sisters meet,
    And each for other's weelfare kindly spiers:
  The social hours, swift-wing'd, unnotic'd fleet;
    Each tells the uncos that he sees or hears;
  The parents, partial, ee their hopefu' years:
    Anticipation forward points the view:
  The *Mother*, wi' her needle and her sheers,
    Gars auld claes look amaist as weel's the new;
  The *Father* mixes a' wi' admonition due.

" Their master's and their mistress's command
    The younkers a' are warned to obey;
  And mind their labours wi' an eydent hand,
    And ne'er, though out o' sight, to jauk or play;

'And, O! be sure to fear the LORD alway!
  And mind your *duty* duly morn and night!
Lest in temptation's path ye gang as'ray,
  Implore his counsel and assisting might:
They never sought in vain that sought the LORD aright.' "

All who have been in a manufacturing town, will recollect the disgusting scenes that are to be witnessed there on a Saturday night.

On Sunday I was much pleased at witnessing the clean, decent, sober, and orderly appearance of the inhabitants of the rural districts, and to see the neighbouring gentry attending the church, preceded or followed by their servants. This was so very different from anything I had been accustomed to before, that it made a lasting impression on my mind.

In a manufacturing town, some, from exhaustion, prefer laying in bed—others are obliged to lay there while the wife washes their clothes; some are strolling about the streets or fields in their working dress, not daring to go to church, for fear of falling asleep; while those who wish to go, and would go if they could, are compelled to labour two or three hours, and getting heated, they must have a glass or two of ale at a public-house to finish with.

The manufacturer and their families attend their place of worship, and wish to be considered patterns of religion and piety; but their pretences and their works are so widely different, that this cloak is easily seen through; for while they are attending meetings for the abolition of slavery, and the propagation of the Scriptures in foreign parts, they are compelling their servants, under fear of losing their situations, to be slaves, and to break the sacred commands of God, at home, even in defiance of the threats of the better sort of the inhabitants, and the public press; and this, too, without fee or reward.

From Portsmouth I came to London. My spirits getting heavier, and my bundle lighter at every stage, and not being able to meet with employment, I suffered considerably from want, visiting any place where I could get a mouthful to eat, and sometimes obliged to walk the streets by night, not being able to pay for a lodging—occasionally resting myself by sitting on the benches in Covent Garden Market, or stretching my weary limbs in the recesses of Westminster Bridge. When in this latter place, I was awoke one morning about two o'clock by the policeman on duty, and obliged to move on, cold, tired, and hungry, I dragged myself along, not knowing or caring where I went, with the dark lowering sky above, and the angry foaming billows beneath; and heaven only knows what would have been the consequence at that critical moment, had I not been sustained by that power which had protected me through all my difficulties.

Soon after this, there was a gentleman wanting a man to improve himself as a tailor and draper; and thinking, from the little knowledge I had acquired in the business at Kendal, and the lameness of my knees, that it would be a suitable situation for me, I applied, and was engaged for three years. For the first twelve months I got on very well; and being desirous to gather a connexion of my own against the time I should begin for myself, I took in little jobs on my own account, which privilege my master allowed me. This brought me in a little money, and was paving the way to a business in future; but I did not then consider that I was over-exerting myself, as I had my own work to do, after my day's work for my master was over, and when I ought to have been in bed.

In the spring of 1840, I began to feel some painful symptoms in my right wrist, arising from the general weakness of my joints, brought on in the factories. At first I was not alarmed at it, as I had occasionally felt similar painful sensations in all my joints for years previous to leaving the factories, and which had always gone off, by taking rest for a day or two, rubbing them with liniment, and wrapping them in warm flannel. But, this time, it resisted all my endeavours to restore strength, the swelling and pain increased; and although I had the advice of some of the most eminent medical practitioners, it was all to no purpose; and, having

F

been off work for a length of time, and my resources failing, I was under the necessity of entering St. Thomas's Hospital, where I remained for upwards of six months; and where every care and attention was paid me, and every expedient tried, that skill and experience could suggest, but with no better success than before. The wrist at this time measured twelve inches round,—and I was worn down to a mere skeleton, not being able to sleep night nor day, except for very short periods, and generally starting up from pain.

It now became pretty evident to all who saw me, that I must, very soon, lose either my hand or my life. A consultation was held by the surgeons of the hospital, who came to the conclusion, that amputation was absolutely necessary; and the result proved their decision to be correct. They gave me a reasonable time to think the matter over—and I decided upon taking their advice.

On the 18th of July, I underwent the operation. The hand being taken off a little below the elbow, in order to clear the affected part of the bone; and thus, another plan to raise myself above want, and keep myself from the workhouse, was frustrated and dashed to the ground! On dissection, the bones of the fore-arm presented a very curious appearance—something similar to an empty honeycomb, the marrow also having totally disappeared; thus accounting at once for the weakness and pain I had occasionally felt in this arm for years, and which, without doubt, may be clearly traced to the same cause as the rest of my sufferings—viz. the factory system.

By the blessing of God, and under the care and attendance of the surgeons and nurses of the hospital, to whom I would ever hope to be thankful, I was restored to tolerable health, and was discharged on the 24th of November, 1840.

It will be necessary here to observe, that in consequence of not being able to meet with employment, I had not paid my contribution-money to the Society of Odd Fellows, and hoping for better days, I did not (as I ought to have done) make my case known; and according to the rules, that I had assisted to make at the annual meeting, I ceased to be a member : however, it is but justice to say, that the members in London behaved very kindly to me.

Having applied to my late master for a certificate of character, I received the following :—

" The bearer, William Dodd, has been in my employ for twelve months, during which time he conducted himself in a sober, honest, and industrious manner ; and I should have taken him again into my service, but for the misfortune of losing his hand, which renders him totally unfit for my business. Given by me this 26th day of November, 1840.

" JOHN KIRBY.

" No. 2, Oldham Place, Bagnige Wells Road, London."

Figure to yourself, dear reader, my deplorable situation at that time—just leaving the hospital, after a residence of six months within its walls, having lost the best part of my right arm !—a cripple in my limbs !—without a home !—without friends !—and with only 8s. in money !—in a strange place, and nearly 300 miles from the place to which I belong !—and, in this condition, to brave the horrors of a severe winter ! and provide myself a living in an unthinking and unfeeling world ! But I put my trust in the Lord, and He has not forsaken me—He has provided me a shelter from the blast, and a crust to satisfy the cravings of nature.

In reading the history of some eastern nations, we find accounts of children having been tied in open baskets to the tops of trees, and there left exposed, an offering to their Gods, till the birds had eaten their flesh from their bones ; and of others having been thrown into the Ganges, and there having found a watery grave—and eagerly, in our exalted ideas of civilization, denounce them as barbarians who could be guilty of such cruelties ! But how much better would it have been for me, if I had had the good fortune to have been so sacrificed in my infancy, rather than have been put to daily torture for upwards of a quarter of a century, and *with the certainty of my miseries still continuing, till my feeble frame sinks beneath its load!*

Think not, dear reader, that I have here drawn an exaggerated picture of a factory life:—it would be well for me if it could be proved that I am wrong—if, instead of being a miserable cripple, scarcely the shadow of a man, it could be proved that I am straight, strong, and hardy as when I entered the factories. But as I feel convinced that this is not possible, it may be well here to say, that I am prepared to prove myself right; and that I shall not hesitate (if required) to wait upon any individual or party, for the purpose of discussing, explaining, illustrating, or proving any of the preceding statements; and further, that I do not shrink from any investigation, but court inquiry.

I would draw the attention of every person who can feel for the miseries of his fellow creatures, to this important subject; and after convincing him of the reality, and the great extent of country over which these evils prevail, ask the following question:—

Is it consistent with the character of this enlightened, Christian country, which has furnished such a proof of her benevolence and charity, in granting 20 millions of money for the abolition of slavery abroad, that we, who have exerted every means in our power in the production of the wealth of the nation, and have therein sacrificed everything valuable in life, that we, the worn-out, cast-off cripples of the manufacturers, should be left to perish and die of want at home?—Forbid it Heaven.

And to you, my fellow sufferers, I would say a word in conclusion. We read in the Scriptures, that God formed man of the dust of the earth, after his own image, breathed into him the breath of life, and endowed him with wonderful powers and faculties; and though these powers and faculties have, in our frames, been injured, rendered nearly useless, and, in many instances, almost destroyed, by our cruel task-masters, yet there still remains that vital principal, over which these earthly tyrants have no power, excepting so far as their evil example extends. It will therefore be our interest to endeavour, by every means in our power, to secure to ourselves this only source of happiness that is left us : and this can only be done by attending to the precepts of the Scriptures. Let us, then, duly appreciate the value of those blessings we do and may enjoy :— let us look abroad and examine the works of our Creator, and we shall soon learn to admire his wisdom, and tremble at his power. We shall learn to despise the riches and pageantry of this perishing scene of things, and fix our hopes on those which are permament and worth our care— to tread with patience the rugged paths of virtue, which will at length conduct us to the happy mansions of eternal repose.

23, *Little Gray's Inn Lane,*
    June 18, 1841.

www.ingramcontent.com/pod-product-compliance
Lightning Source LLC
Chambersburg PA
CBHW081304040426
42452CB00014B/2645